P9-DSZ-218

Scott Foresman

Scott Foresman
Reading
Surprise Me!

Good Times We Share

Take a Closer Look

Let's Learn Together

Favorite Things Old and New

Take Me There

Surprise Me!

Scott
Foresman

About the Cover Artist

Maryjane Begin and her family live in Providence, Rhode Island, where she teaches college students when she is not working on her own art. Many of her illustrations—even imaginary places—show how things in Providence look.

Cover illustration © Maryjane Begin

ISBN 0-328-03932-2

Copyright © 2004, Pearson Education, Inc.

All Rights Reserved. Printed in the United States of America. This publication is protected by Copyright and permission should be obtained from the publisher prior to any prohibited reproduction, storage in a retrieval system, or transmission in any form by any means, electronic, mechanical, photocopying, recording, or likewise. For information regarding permission(s), write to: Permissions Department, Scott Foresman, 1900 East Lake Avenue, Glenview, Illinois 60025.

3 4 5 6 7 8 9 10 V063 10 09 08 07 06 05 04 03 02

Scott Foresman
Reading
Surprise Me!

Program Authors

Peter Afflerbach

James Beers

Camille Blachowicz

Candy Dawson Boyd

Wendy Cheyney

Deborah Diffily

Dolores Gaunty-Porter

Connie Juel

Donald Leu

Jeanne Paratore

Sam Sebesta

Karen Kring Wixson

Scott
Foresman

Editorial Offices: Glenview, Illinois • Parsippany, New Jersey • New York, New York
Sales Offices: Parsippany, New Jersey • Duluth, Georgia • Glenview, Illinois
Coppell, Texas • Ontario, California

Contents

Unit 6

Unit 6

7

Surprise Me!

How do we get all those great ideas?

Bluebirds in the Garden

by Deborah Eaton
illustrated by Meg Aubrey

My name is Cheyenne. Come see my garden. It's out here, in my yard. Do you know what I'm growing? It is **not** flowers! It is **not** something to eat! It's something much more fun. Shall I tell you?

I'm growing birdhouses. Really I am!

I started last year. I put seeds in jars. I waited a long time. Suddenly, little green plants came up. I could hardly see them. But they were there!

Pretty soon, my plants got much too big for the jars. So I had to dig a hole for them.

Digging was hard work! But you know what? It wasn't nearly as hard as waiting!

I could hardly stand it!
I wish, wish, wish birdhouses didn't
grow so slowly!

After a long time, they got big.
They got yellow flowers. Then the
stems near the flowers got dark
green and started to swell. I knew
those parts would be birdhouses!
They got big and fat like these.

See? I really did grow birdhouses!
I picked them and let them dry.
Then my dad got to work. He cut
holes for the birds to go in and out.

I got out my art stuff. I painted
them. It was fun!

One large plant had a lot of seeds.
I gave the seeds to my friends to
plant.

Now just look at these! All that
work really paid off!

Soon all our yards will be filled
with birds. Bluebirds! That's what I
want. I can hardly wait.

The Garden

by Arnold Lobel

Frog was in his garden.
Toad came walking by.
"What a fine garden
you have, Frog," he said.

"Yes," said Frog. "It is very
nice, but it was hard work."

"I wish I had a garden,"
said Toad.

"Here are some flower seeds.
Plant them in the ground," said
Frog, "and soon you will have
a garden."

"How soon?" asked Toad.

"Quite soon," said Frog.

Toad ran home.

He planted the flower seeds.

"Now seeds," said Toad,

"start growing."

Toad walked up and down

a few times.

The seeds did not start to grow.

Toad put his head close to the
ground and said loudly,
"Now seeds, start growing!"

Toad looked at the ground again.
The seeds did not start to grow.

21

Toad put his head very
close to the ground and shouted,
"NOW SEEDS, START GROWING!"

Frog came running up the path.
"What is all this noise?" he asked.

"My seeds will not grow," said Toad.

"You are shouting too much,"
said Frog. "These poor seeds
are afraid to grow."

"My seeds are afraid to grow?"
asked Toad.

"Of course," said Frog.

"Leave them alone for a few days.

Let the sun shine on them,

let the rain fall on them.

Soon your seeds will start to grow."

That night Toad looked out
of his window.
"Drat!" said Toad.
"My seeds have not started to
grow. They must be afraid of
the dark."

Toad went out to his garden
with some candles.
"I will read the seeds a story,"
said Toad. "Then they will
not be afraid."

Toad read a long story
to his seeds.

All the next day
Toad sang songs
to his seeds.

And all the next day
Toad read poems
to his seeds.

And all the next day
Toad played music
for his seeds.

Toad looked at the ground.
The seeds still did not
start to grow.
"What shall I do?" cried Toad.
"These must be the most
frightened seeds in the
whole world!"

Then Toad felt very tired,
and he fell asleep.

"Toad, Toad, wake up," said Frog.
"Look at your garden!"

Toad looked at his garden.
Little green plants were coming
up out of the ground.

"At last," shouted Toad,
"my seeds have stopped
being afraid to grow!"

"And now you will have
a nice garden too," said Frog.

"Yes," said Toad,
"but you were right, Frog.
It was very hard work."

About the Author and Illustrator

Arnold Lobel

"There is a little world at the end of my pencil," said Arnold Lobel about writing books. He wrote almost one hundred books. His Frog and Toad books are the most well known.

Mr. Lobel watched his children catch frogs and toads. That gave him ideas for the Frog and Toad stories.

Field Row
by Alma Flor Ada

In the field row
lies a seed, all tucked in
like a baby in the crib.
Sleep tight today, seed.
Wake up tomorrow, plant.

Surco
por Alma Flor Ada

En el surco
la semilla arropada
como el niñito en la cuna.
Duérmete, semilla, hoy.
Despierta, planta, mañana.

Reader Response

Let's Talk

Toad sang songs and read poems to his seeds. What would you do to help seeds grow?

Let's Think

Do you think Toad's seeds really were afraid to grow? Why or why not?

Test Prep

Let's Write

Cheyenne and Toad both grew things. Which story taught you more about growing things? Write sentences to tell why you think so.

Grow a Design

You can plant a design and watch it grow.

What you need:

alfalfa seeds   spray bottle   soil
foil cake pans   pencils

What you do:

1. Use your pencil to poke holes in the bottom of a foil pan.
2. Sprinkle about one inch of soil in the pan.
3. Draw a design in the soil.
4. Drop seeds into your design.
5. Cover your seeds with a little more soil.
6. Spray the soil with water every day.
7. Soon you will see your design grow.

Read Together
Language Arts

Sentences

A sentence tells a complete idea.

It has a naming part and an action part.

A sentence begins with a capital letter.

Some sentences tell.

Telling sentences end with a **.** .

Paul grows flowers and berries **.**

Some sentences ask questions.

Questions end with a **?** .

What does Paul grow in his garden**?**

Talk

Look at the picture. Use a telling sentence to tell something about it. Use a question to ask something.

Write

Write the sentences correctly. Use capital letters and a **.** or **?** .

1. what color are the berries

2. the boy uses a hoe

3. do you like sunflowers

Write your own telling sentence and question. Remember to use capital letters and a **.** or **?** .

Jordan Makes a New Friend

by David A. Adler

illustrated by C. D. Hullinger

Jordan looked outside. Snow was coming down. Wind was blowing the snow off the walk into large drifts.

"Mark called," Jordan's mother said. "He can't get here in the storm."

Jordan said, "But Mark told me he would come. I like playing with him. We play games. He likes my stories. He's good at sharing."

When the snow stopped falling and the wind stopped blowing, Jordan went outside. He made a snow fort and a snowman. He named the snowman Mort.

He gave Mort an old scarf so Mort would not get cold.

Jordan and Mort played
Hide and Seek. Jordan found
Mort every time, but Mort
never found Jordan.

Jordan told Mort a story.
Mort liked it. Jordan made
two snow cones. One for
him and one for Mort.
    Mort let Jordan have his.

Jordan's mother said, "Come inside. It's cold. Your coat and hat are full of snow."

Before Jordan went in, he said to Mort,
"We played games. You liked my story.
You are good at sharing, just like Mark."
"I am?" someone said.
Jordan jumped. "Mort, you can talk!"

"It's me," Mark said. He stepped
out from behind Mort. "The snowstorm
stopped, so here I am."

"I'm glad you came," Jordan said
as they went inside. "Playing with
Mort was fun. Playing with you will
be even better."

Ice-Cold Birthday

by Maryann Cocca-Leffler

Some people have all the luck!
I have luck too.
Bad luck.
The week before the dance show,
I broke my arm.

The year I held
the flag in the
parade, it rained.

And the day of
our class pictures,
I spilled green
paint all over my
new dress.
But on my birthday
I was sure my luck
would change.

My birthday
started out great.
It was snowing!
Everything looked
so pretty.

Dad made a
birthday pancake.
It was a seven.

At school I got an A in math.
But the best part was still to come.
Six friends were coming to my party.

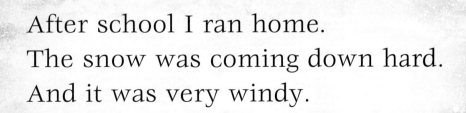

After school I ran home.
The snow was coming down hard.
And it was very windy.

Mom was baking a big cake.
Dad was blowing up balloons.
My sister set the table with
party plates and candy.
What a great party this was
going to be.

Then I heard the radio . . .

~BAD STORM IS HERE~
~TWO FEET OF SNOW~
~HIGH WINDS~

"Oh no! My party!" I said.

"Don't worry," said Dad.
"With luck the storm will pass."

Luck? I have no luck!

That's when it happened.
The radio stopped playing.
The cake stopped baking.
All the lights went off.
The power was out.
Then the calls came.
No one could come
to my party.

"I knew it!
I knew it!"
I cried.

I put on my coat.
I sat down and
stared at the
blank TV.
No cake.
No party.
No fun.
Just an ice-cold
birthday!

Then Mom came in.
She had a funny cake.
It was made of ice cream
and cookies.
I had to smile.
I made a wish and blew
out the candles.

We ate my cake.
Then Dad held the flashlight.
We made shadow puppets.

Later, everybody played pin-the-tail-on-the-donkey.
It was so dark.
Nobody needed blindfolds.

Then Mom told a spooky story.
It was about Iceman.
I had to admit it.
I was having fun.

The best part was when
Mom and Dad brought
in my big surprise.
It was a brand-new sled!
It had stopped snowing.
So we all went sledding.

The moon was full.
And snow, snow, snow
was everywhere.
Up and down the hill we went.
When it got too cold,
we started back home.

We got to the front yard.
"Look!" said Dad.
He wrote "Happy Birthday"
in the snow.
"That's the biggest card
you will ever get!"

"Lucky for me, it snowed!" I said.
Then I heard my words.
Maybe I don't have such bad luck
after all.

About the Author
and Illustrator

Maryann Cocca-Leffler

Many of Maryann Cocca-Leffler's books tell stories of things that really happened. "The idea for the ice-cream cookie cake in *Ice-Cold Birthday* came from a cake we made for my sister when we forgot her birthday," says Ms. Cocca-Leffler.

Ms. Cocca-Leffler dedicated her book to her sister. She wrote, "For my sister Diane, may you never go without a real birthday cake again!"

Sunflakes

by Frank Asch

If sunlight fell like snowflakes,
gleaming yellow and so bright,
we could build a sunman,
we could have a sunball fight,
we could watch the sunflakes
drifting in the sky.

We could go sleighing

in the middle of July

through sundrifts and sunbanks,

we could ride a sunmobile,

and we could touch sunflakes—

I wonder how they'd feel.

Reader Response

Let's Talk

The girl's family turned a bad day into a good day. What did you like best about the girl's birthday? Why?

Let's Think

On page 53 the girl said, "Luck? I have no luck!" Why did she say this? Do you agree with her?

Test Prep

Let's Write

What did the girl and her family do to make the stormy day fun? What can you do for fun on a stormy day? Make a list.

A Stormy Day Game

You can make and play a game called **Make a Face.**

1. Draw the shape of a head on heavy paper. Cut it out. Tape the head to an easel or chalkboard.

2. Cut out a nose, a mouth, two ears, a hat, and hair. Add a strip of tape to the top of each part.

3. Ask each player to choose a part.

4. Blindfold a player. Ask him or her to tape the part where it belongs.

5. The winner is the player whose part is in the right spot.

Language Arts

Exclamations

An **exclamation** is a sentence that shows strong feelings. An exclamation begins with a capital letter. It ends with an **!** .

Here comes the parade**!**

Talk

Tell something you like to do with your family. Make it sound like an exclamation.

74

Write

Write the exclamations correctly.
Use capital letters and an **!** .

1. we love a circus parade

2. the clowns are so funny

3. acrobats are very brave

Write your own exclamations.
Remember to use capital
letters and an **!** .

Show Time
Your First Play
by Phyllis Root

What do you need to put on a play?
First, you need a play. You can find
one in a book. Or you can make one
up. Once you have a play, everyone
needs to work together.

Who will play the parts? Some actors may be taller. Other actors may be smaller. Who will be best for each part? Which person or animal do you want to play?

You may need to make costumes.
Ask a grown-up for things you can use.
A fur coat turns you into a bear. A big
red shirt turns you into a bird.

You can make props too. Boxes make good props. You can even paint the boxes. A smaller box can be a chair. A bigger box can be a table. The biggest box can be a bed.

Now you need to learn your part.
First say your lines over and over. Say
them to each other. Do you need to
speak faster or slower?

Who will come to your play? Ask your family. Ask your friends. Put up posters that say SEE THE BIGGEST SHOW UNDER THE SUN.

At last it's time for your play. Once the play starts, don't stop. You can help each other out if someone forgets a line. The show must go on!

When the play is over, say "Thank you" when people clap. Your play will be the best! Have a party after the play. Then plan another big show.

Do You Live in a Nest?

by Carmen Tafolla

illustrated by Lee Lee Brazeal

CHARACTERS

CRICKET

FROG

TURTLE

DOG

HORSE

LION

BIRD

FROG: Hi, Cricket!

CRICKET: Frog! Frog! Bird is coming to visit.

FROG: I am happy to hear that. Bird makes the sweetest sounds.

CRICKET: Where will she stay?

FROG: She can stay with me!

CRICKET: Do you live in a nest?

FROG: No, I live in a nice, wet pond. There are lots of flies to eat! Once Bird is here, she can pick which fly she wants.

CRICKET: I do not think Bird wants a pond. She needs some place warmer than that.

TURTLE: Hi, Cricket! Hi, Frog!

CRICKET: Turtle! Turtle! Bird is coming to visit!

TURTLE: I am happy to hear that. Bird makes the
          sweetest sounds.

CRICKET: Where will she stay?

TURTLE: She can stay with me!

CRICKET: Do you live in a nest?

TURTLE: No, I live in a flat field near the pond. It has nice, green grass! Once Bird is here, she can eat all the grass she wants.

CRICKET: I do not think Bird wants a field. She needs some place rounder than that.

DOG: Hi, Cricket! Hi, Frog! Hi, Turtle!

CRICKET: Dog! Dog! Bird is coming to visit!

DOG: I am happy to hear that. Bird makes the sweetest sounds.

CRICKET: Where will she stay?

DOG: She can stay with me!

CRICKET: Do you live in a nest?

DOG: No, I sleep on the ground under a big tree. There are lots of bones hidden under the tree! Once Bird is here, she can pick which bone she wants.

CRICKET: I do not think Bird wants to sleep on the ground. She needs some place higher than that.

HORSE: Hi, Cricket! Hi, Frog! Hi, Turtle! Hi, Dog!

CRICKET: Horse! Horse! Bird is coming to visit!

HORSE: I am happy to hear that. Bird makes the sweetest sounds.

CRICKET: Where will she stay?

HORSE: She can stay with me!

CRICKET: Do you live in a nest?

HORSE: No, I live in a nice big barn. There are many bundles of hay! Once Bird is here, she can pick any bundle she wants.

CRICKET: I do not think Bird wants a barn. She needs some place smaller than that.

LION: Roar!

CRICKET: Lion! Bird is coming to visit.

LION: I am happy to hear that. Bird makes the sweetest sounds.

CRICKET: Where will she stay?

LION: I am the king. I do not like other animals in my way, but Bird is a visitor. She can stay with me!

CRICKET: Do you live in a nest?

LION: No, I live on a great big rock. There are lots of rabbits around to chase! Once Bird is here, she can pick which rabbit she wants.

CRICKET: I do not think Bird wants a rock. She needs some place softer than that.

LION: You're right. Bird needs some place softer.

HORSE: She needs some place smaller.

DOG: She needs some place higher.

TURTLE: She needs some place rounder.

FROG: She needs some place warmer.

CRICKET: Bird needs a nest!

LION: Horse, what are you doing?

HORSE: I am getting some hay. We are going to build a nest for her.

TURTLE: Thank you for the hay, Horse. But how can we make a nest?

DOG: I can roll the hay and make it round.
I love to play with a ball.

FROG: Turtle, what are you doing?

TURTLE: I can pat a warm place in the hay
for Bird.

DOG: Thank you, Turtle. It is a great nest.

LION: Where do we put it?

CRICKET: I know where we can find the tallest tree!

LION: How do we get it up in the tree?

FROG: Lion, pick it up with your claws. Put it on my back. I will jump up into the tree. I will put Bird's nest on the highest branch.

BIRD: Cricket! Cricket! I've come to visit!

CRICKET: We have a nest for you! Do you like it?

BIRD: Oh, it's the softest, smallest, highest, roundest, warmest nest of all! Which one of you made the nest?

HORSE: We all helped each other. Now we can help each other do one more thing.

ALL: Yes! Let's have a party!

The First Grade's Play

Mrs. Cruz's class put on the play *Do You Live in a Nest?* The children sold tickets. They made this chart to show how many tickets they sold each day.

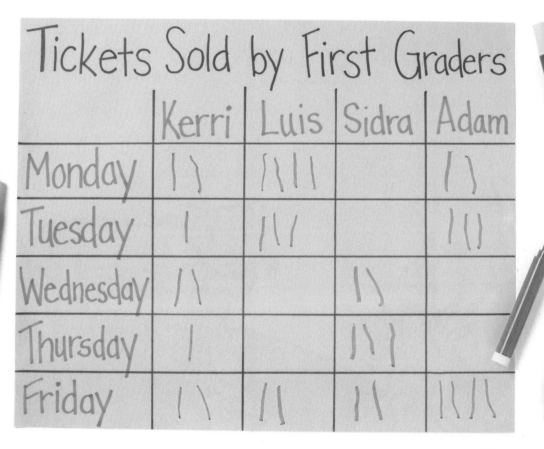

Tickets Sold by First Graders	Kerri	Luis	Sidra	Adam
Monday	I I	I\ I I		I I
Tuesday	I	I\ I		I \ I
Wednesday	I\		I I	
Thursday	I		I\ I	
Friday	I \	I I	I I	I\ I \

Let's Talk

Who sold tickets every day?
On which day did the children
sell the most tickets?

About the Author

Carmen Tafolla

When Carmen Tafolla was a little girl, her Aunt Esther told her a bedtime story about an ant. That story gave Dr. Tafolla the idea for *Do You Live in a Nest?* Dr. Tafolla wrote her play about a cricket, not an ant. But one thing she kept the same. The animals in both work together to make everyone happy.

Reader Response

Let's Talk

Which animal in the play do you think is most helpful? Why?

Let's Think

What is the problem in the story? How is it solved?

Test Prep

Let's Write

Look back in the story. Write the steps the animals took to make the nest. Use words such as *first, next, then,* and *last.*

Put on a Play

Follow these steps to put on the play
called *Do You Live in a Nest?*

1. Choose someone to say the name of the
   play and tell who is in it.
2. Choose who will read the parts of Frog,
   Cricket, Turtle, Dog, Horse, Lion, and Bird.
3. Practice reading sentences with **?** and **!**
   at the end. How does your voice sound?
4. Read your part so that everyone
   can hear.

Language Arts

Commands

A command is a sentence that tells someone to do something. A command begins with a capital letter. It ends with a **.** .

Walk slowly in the halls**.**

Talk

Look at the pictures. What commands might you give the children in the play?

Write

Write the commands correctly. Use capital letters and a **.** .

1. hand the crown to the king

2. help the queen sit on her throne

3. close the curtains now

Write your own commands. Remember to use capital letters and a **.** .

What's New in Mrs. Powell's Class?

by Anne Sibley O'Brien
illustrated by Gil Ashby

"It's newsletter time," Mrs. Powell told her class. "What can we tell parents about?"
"The trip to the farm," said Jason.
"And don't forget about the cows running away!" said Danny.

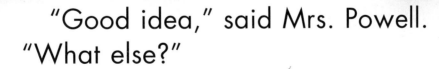

"Good idea," said Mrs. Powell.
"What else?"

"The play," said Lola, "so lots
of people will come see us."

"Great!" said Mrs. Powell. "Now
let's get to work."

Mrs. Powell's Class News

Mr. Brown's Farm

We went on a field trip to see Mr. Brown's cows. Mariko forgot to pull the gate shut. All the cows got out. Mr. Brown had to chase them down the road and along the river.

We want to thank Mr. Brown and his
cows for a great time. Danny said
it really was a field trip because
the cows were in the field. Ha ha.

A Funny Play

Please come to our class play on Monday at 2:00. It tells how a jester saves a town from a dragon. He goes to the dragon and tells riddles. The dragon likes the riddles better than scaring people.

Lola is the queen. She wears a crown and a fancy gown.

Jason is a scary dragon. He prowls along the wall.

Danny likes to be funny, so he is the jester. This play will make you howl.

Fox on Stage

by James Marshall

One Saturday morning
Fox and his friends were
just lying around.

"What a sad little group,"
said Mom.
"Why don't you *do* something?"

"The television is broken,"
said Fox.

"Oh, that *is* terrible!"
said Mom.

Then Fox had one of his
great ideas.

"Let's put on a play!" he said.
"We can charge everyone a dime."

"We'll get rich!" said Dexter.

"I'll buy a new car," said Carmen.

And they went to the library.

"Let's do a spooky play," said Carmen.
"We can scare all the little kids."

"Here's what you need," said Miss Pencil.
"It's called *Spooky Plays*.
My favorite is 'The Mummy's Toe.'"

"Oooh," said the gang.

Fox and the gang went home to practice.

"The Mummy's Toe" was *very* scary.

Dexter played the mummy.

Carmen was the princess.

And Fox was the hero.

Soon things were moving right along.

Fox and Dexter worked hard
on the set.

And Carmen put up posters
all over town.

Mom and Louise helped out
with the costumes.

"Hold still," said Mom.

"I hope I'm scary enough," said Dexter.
It was time for the play.

Fox peeked out from behind the curtain.
There was a big crowd.

"I hope everything goes okay,"
said Dexter.

"What could go wrong?" said Fox.

The curtain went up.

And the play began.

Right away Carmen forgot her lines.

"Well, I *did* know them," she said to
the audience.

Then Dexter crashed through
the scenery.

"Whoops," said Dexter.

It was Fox's turn to appear.

Suddenly it began to rain.
Fox's beautiful paper costume
fell apart in front of everyone.

"What do we do now?" said Carmen.

"Pull the curtain down!"

Fox called out to Louise.

And Louise pulled with all her might.

The curtain came down.

"Who turned out the lights?"
cried Carmen.

"Where am I?" said Dexter.

"The play is ruined!" cried Fox.
"*Everything* went wrong!"

The next day Fox heard
some folks talking.

"That Fox really knows how to put on a funny show," someone said.

"Funniest thing I ever saw," said someone else.

And Fox began to plan his next show.

About the Author and Illustrator

James Marshall wrote many books about friendship. He added drawings to show friends together. Mr. Marshall wrote eleven books about Fox and his friends.

"You have to make a book *move*," Mr. Marshall said about writing. "There always has to be a reason to turn to the next page." He always tried to add a really special ending. Does "Fox on Stage" have one of those endings?

Reader Response

Let's Talk

There is a mummy, a princess, and a hero in Fox's play. Which part would you want to play? Why?

Let's Think

Why does Fox think his play is ruined? What made him decide to do another one?

Test Prep
Let's Write

Carmen makes a poster for "The Mummy's Toe." Some information is missing. Write what Carmen should put on her poster.

Make a Poster

You can make a poster for Fox's next play.

1. Make up a name for the play.
2. Tell where and when it will take place. Tell who is in it.
3. Draw something that will make people want to come.

129

Language Arts

Pronouns

A **pronoun** is a word that can take the place of a noun. These words are pronouns.

I	**you**	**he**	**she**	**it**
we	**you**	**they**		

Jan wants to fly the ship.
She wants to fly the ship.

What word does **She** take the place of?

Talk

Tell something you see happening in the picture. First, use a child's name in the sentence. Then use a pronoun in place of the name.

Write

Write the sentences using a pronoun in place of each name. Draw a line under the pronouns.

1. P.J. makes a new friend.

2. Annie collects rocks.

3. Dad and Mom are going to Mars.

Write a sentence about yourself and a friend. Use pronouns in place of your names.

Doggy Art

by David McPhail

One day Jill painted a picture.
Then she went outside to play.
She left her paints on the living
room floor.

Along came Jill's dog, Rudy.
Rudy sat down beside the paints.
His tail was in the paint. Rudy
wagged his tail. His tail painted a
picture.

Rudy thought painting was fun. Rudy painted another picture. There was no more paper, so he painted on the rug.

Rudy kept painting. He painted a flower on a chair.

After that, he painted a tree and
some clouds on the sofa. When Jill's
mother came home, Rudy went out.
Jill's mother went into the living room.
What she found almost made her shout.

Jill came in. "Do you like my
painting?" she asked her mother.

"Did you paint the rug?" asked
Jill's mother. "And the sofa and the
chair?"

"No," Jill said, "just this picture."

Jill's mother went to the door.
"Rudy!" she called.

Rudy came into the house. Rudy
was covered with paint.

"Now I know who painted the
rug and the chair and the sofa,"
Jill's mother said.

"Maybe Rudy thinks he is an
artist," said Jill.
"Maybe," thought Jill's mother,
and she laughed. Jill laughed too.

Then she helped her mother
clean the living room. Jill knew Rudy
needed cleaning too. So after that,
Rudy took a bath.

The Snow Glory

by Cynthia Rylant
illustrated by Suçie Stevenson

When the snow melted
and spring came,
Henry and his dog Mudge
stayed outside
all the time.

Henry had missed
riding his bike.
Mudge had missed
chewing on sticks.
They were glad
it was warmer.

One day when Henry and Mudge

were in their yard,

Henry saw something blue

on the ground.

He got closer to it.

"Mudge!" he called.

"It's a flower!"

Mudge slowly walked over

and sniffed the blue flower.

Then he sneezed
all over Henry.

"Aw, Mudge," Henry said.

Later, Henry's mother
told him that the flower
was called a snow glory.

"Can I pick it?"
Henry asked.

"Oh, no," said his mother.
"Let it grow."

So Henry didn't pick it.

Every day he saw the snow glory

in the yard,

blue

and looking so pretty.

He knew he shouldn't pick it.

He was trying not to pick it.

But he thought how nice

it would look in a jar.

He thought how nice

to bring it inside.

He thought how nice

it would be

to own that snow glory.

Every day he stood with Mudge

and looked at the flower.

Mudge would stick his nose

into the grass

all around the snow glory.

But he never looked at it

the way Henry did.

"Don't you think the snow glory

has been growing long enough?"

Henry would ask his mother.

"Let it grow, Henry,"

she would say.

Oh, Henry wanted that snow glory.

And one day

he just knew

he had to have it.

So he took Mudge

by the collar

and he stood

beside the snow glory.

"I'm going to pick it,"

Henry whispered to Mudge.

"I've let it grow a long time."

Henry bent his head and

he said in Mudge's ear,

"Now I *need* it."

And Mudge wagged his tail,

licked Henry's face,

then put his big mouth

right over that snow glory . . .

and he ate it.

"No, Mudge!" Henry said.

But too late.

There was a blue flower
in Mudge's belly.

"I said *need* it, not *eat* it!"

shouted Henry.

He was so mad because

Mudge took his flower.

It was Henry's flower

and Mudge took it.

And Henry almost said,
"Bad dog," but he stopped.
He looked at Mudge,
who looked back at him
with soft brown eyes
and a flower in his belly.

Henry knew it wasn't his snow glory.

He knew it wasn't anybody's snow glory.

Just a thing to let grow.

And if someone ate it,

it was just a thing to let go.

Henry stopped feeling mad.

He put his arms around

Mudge's big head.

"Next time, Mudge,"

he said,

"try to *listen* better."

Mudge wagged his tail

and licked his lips.

One blue petal

fell from his mouth

into Henry's hand.

Henry smiled,

put it in his pocket,

and they went inside.

About the Author

Cynthia Rylant once worked as a children's librarian. After reading children's books, she knew that she wanted to write for children.

Caring for her son, Nate, and two dogs gave her the idea for her Henry and Mudge stories. "I know about cold shivers, big tests, happy cats, and wild winds," she says. "And especially big drooly lovable dogs."

About the Illustrator

Suçie Stevenson has done all the drawings for the Henry and Mudge books. She has also written her own books.

Ms. Stevenson lives with two dogs too. Sometimes her dogs are right under her desk while she works. "If I ever forget how Mudge would act, I just look under my desk," she says.

Reader Response

Let's Talk

Think about Rudy in "Doggy Art" and Mudge in "The Snow Glory." Each dog did something he shouldn't. Which mistake do you think was harder to fix? Why?

Let's Think

Why doesn't Henry stay mad at Mudge after Mudge eats the flower?

Test Prep

Let's Write

"The Snow Glory" is about a boy and his dog. What books have you read about a dog or some other pet? Write a book report about one. Tell the title and author and why you like it.

Make a Paper Flower

What you need:

soft paper

small wire

What you do:

1

Fold three sheets of soft paper in half.

2

Wrap a small wire around the soft paper.

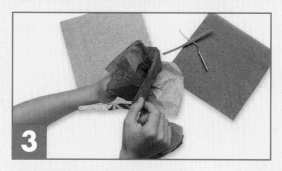

3

Unfold the paper.

4

Use the flower to tell the story of Henry and Mudge.

Language Arts

Pronouns

Pronouns take the place of nouns. Use these pronouns in the naming part of a sentence.

I   he   she   we   they

Use these pronouns in the action part of a sentence.

me   him   her   us   them

Henry fed **the ducks.**

He fed **them.**

What word does **He** take the place of?

What word does **them** take the place of?

Talk

Look at the pictures. Say sentences with pronouns in the naming parts. Say sentences with pronouns in the action parts.

Write

Write the sentences. Circle the nouns in the naming part and in the action part. Draw a line under the pronouns that take the place of the nouns.

1. **The people like the garden. They like it.**
2. **Children feed the ducks. They feed them.**

Write two sentences. In the first sentence use nouns in the naming part and in the action part. In the second sentence, use pronouns in place of the nouns.

I'll Join You

by Juanita Havill
illustrated by Michele Noiset

"My dad says we might move,"
said Erin.

"Where will you go?" said Moy.

"Dad didn't say," said Erin.

"You are my best friend," said
Moy. "Somehow I'll join you."

"What if I move downtown? Then I'll go to another school," said Erin.

"I'll open my piggy bank. I'll grab some coins to pay for the bus," said Moy. "I'll ride downtown and join you at your new school."

"What if I move across the river?" said Erin.

"I'll pack my suitcase with toys and go across in a big boat. I'll enjoy the ride to the other side," said Moy. "We'll always be friends."

"What if I move across the mountains?" said Erin.

"I'll go up the slope. Then I'll ski downhill to the other side," said Moy. "We'll always be friends."

"What if I move across the sea to China?" said Erin.

"I'll become a pilot. I'll fly my airplane to China," said Moy. "We'll always be friends."

"What if I move to the moon?" said Erin.

"I'll become an astronaut. I'll fly to the moon in my spaceship," said Moy. "We'll always be friends."

"Hi, girls!" Erin's dad said. "Did Erin tell you we are moving, Moy?"

"Yes," said Moy. "I'll join her wherever she goes— downtown, across the river, over the mountains, across the sea, or to the moon."

"You won't have to go so far,"
said Erin's dad. "We are moving to
the townhouse across the street."
Erin opened her eyes wide.
Moy said, "Oh, boy!"
Both girls shouted for joy, "Yes!"

LEON and BOB

by Simon James

Leon had moved into town

with his mom.

His dad was away in the army.

Leon shared his room

with his new friend, Bob.

No one else could see Bob,
but Leon knew he was there.
Leon always laid a place
for Bob at the table.
"More milk, Bob?" Leon said.

Sometimes Leon's mom
couldn't take Leon to school,
but Leon didn't mind.
He always walked to school with Bob.
He always had Bob to talk to.

Often, when Leon got home,
there was a letter waiting for him
from his dad.
Bob liked to hear Leon read it
over and over again.

One Saturday, Leon heard

some noises in the street below.

He saw a new family moving in next door.

A boy looked up at Leon and waved.

Leon waved back.

That night Leon kept thinking
about the boy next door.
He decided to go by there
in the morning.
"But you'll have to come with
me, Bob," he said.

The next day Leon and Bob

ate their breakfast

very quickly.

Then Leon grabbed his ball

and rushed outside.

Leon ran up the steps

of the house next door.

He was about halfway

when suddenly he realized

Bob wasn't there anymore.

Leon sat down.

He was all alone.

He could ring the bell

or he could go home.

Why wasn't Bob there

to help him?

Leon rang the bell and waited.

The door opened.

"Hello," said the boy.

"H-hello," said Leon.

"Would you like to go to the park?"

"Okay," said the boy.

"I'm just going to the park, Mom,"
he called.

Together Leon and the boy walked
down the steps toward the street.

"My name's Leon," said Leon.
"What's yours?"

"Bob," said Bob.

About the Author and Illustrator

Simon James lives in England where he writes books and teaches art to children. Mr. James had fourteen jobs before he went to art school and became an author.

He says that he wants the idea for a book to come to him "on its own."

Making Friends

by Eloise Greenfield

when I was in kindergarten
this new girl came in our class one day
and the teacher told her to sit beside me
and I didn't know what to say
so I wiggled my nose and made my bunny face

and she laughed
then she puffed out her cheeks
and she made a funny face
and I laughed
so then
we were friends

Reader Response

Let's Talk

Leon has a friend only he can see. They eat breakfast and walk to school together. What would you do with such a friend?

Let's Think

Why do you think Leon makes up his friend named Bob?

Test Prep

Let's Write

Pretend you are Leon. Write a friendly letter to your made-up friend Bob. Tell him about things you two could do together.

Make a class art gallery of things friends do together.

1. Draw a picture of something you like to do with a friend.

2. Write a sentence about what your picture shows.

3. You can glue macaroni around the picture for a frame.

4. Hang the pictures around the room.

Andy and I make a tent.

Language Arts

Nouns for One or More than One

A noun can mean one or more than one.

Add **-s** or **-es** to mean more than one.

Add **-es** to nouns that end in **x, s, ch,** or **sh.**

> Tim can play with the moving **boxes.**
> Lilly can pretend the **boxes** are **buses.**

Talk

Name the nouns for one in the picture.
Tell the word for more than one.

Write

Write the sentences. Draw one line under the nouns that mean one. Draw two lines under the nouns that mean more than one.

1. **Pack blocks in the boxes.**
2. **The dishes go in this box.**
3. **When can Dad stop for lunch?**

Write your own sentences. Use nouns from the box. You may add **-s** or **-es**. Draw one line under nouns for one. Draw two lines under nouns for more than one.

Nouns

friend

street

ball

bunch

truck

bench

Vocabulary Review

Words I Know

Bluebirds in the Garden

The Garden

ground
much
shall
these
wish
work

Show Time: Your First Play

Do You Live in a Nest?

each
once
other
under
which

Jordan Makes a New Friend

Ice-Cold Birthday

before
cold
full
off
would

What's New in Mrs. Powell's Class?

Fox on Stage

along
goes
great
idea
pull

I'll Join You

LEON and BOB

always
boy
move
open
school

Doggy Art

The Snow Glory

almost
knew
picture
thought
took

Test Talk

Complete the Sentence

A test may show an incomplete sentence. You must choose the answer that correctly completes the sentence.

A test about *Ice-Cold Birthday* might ask you to complete this sentence.

1. **No one came to the party because _____.**

Ⓐ there was another party

Ⓑ the family went sledding

Ⓒ there was a snowstorm

Read the sentence. What do you need to find out? You need to find out *why* no one came to the party. Which answer tells you *why*?

Here is how one boy chose his answer.

I need to find out why no one came to the party. The story didn't tell about another party. The family did go sledding, but that isn't why no one came. There was a snowstorm, so I'll mark C.

Try it!

Which answer would you choose to complete this sentence about *Ice-Cold Birthday*?

2. The thing the girl liked best about her birthday was _____.

(A) watching it snow

(B) eating in the dark

(C) having fun with her family

Glossary

Aa

actors Actors are people who act in a play or in movies and television.

actors

admit To **admit** something is to say that it is true. She **admitted** that I was right.

appear To **appear** means to come in sight. Stars **appear** in the sky at night.

army An **army** is a large group of soldiers.

Bb

beautiful Beautiful means that something we see or hear is very pretty. That was a **beautiful** song.

behind Behind means in back of. The band marched **behind** the leader.

behind

200

birds   Birds have feathers, wings, and two legs. Most **birds** can fly.

blindfolds   Blindfolds are pieces of cloth that cover the eyes. The players in the game all wore **blindfolds.**

brought   If you **brought** something, you carried it with you. We **brought** presents to the party.

brought

bundles   Bundles are things tied up together. We carried **bundles** of newspapers.

Cc

candles   Candles are sticks of wax with a string in their center. **Candles** give light as they burn.

change   Change means to become different. Leaves **change** color in the fall.

charge   To **charge** means to ask as a price. The store **charges** two dollars for milk.

charge

closer Closer means nearer. If you move the book **closer** to me, I can read along.

costumes Costumes are clothes that you can put on to look like someone else. **Costumes** are worn in plays or just for fun.

costumes

cricket A **cricket** is an insect. The male **cricket** makes a loud noise by rubbing its front wings together.

Dd

decided If you have **decided**, you have chosen or made up your mind. Kim **decided** to eat the apple, not the cookie.

Ee

enough There is **enough** food for everyone. Have you eaten **enough?**

eyes The **eyes** are the parts of the body that help you see. Your **eyes** are in your face.

Ff

flowers Flowers are parts of plants. Roses and tulips are **flowers.**

folks Folks is another word for people.

flowers

frightened If you are **frightened**, you are scared or afraid. Al's cat was **frightened** by the dog mask.

frightened

Gg

great **Great** means very big or large. A **great** cloud of smoke rose over the fire.

ground **Ground** means the soil or dirt on the Earth. We planted seeds in the **ground.**

group A **group** is a number of persons or things together. One **group** of children played ball, and another **group** jumped rope.

Jj

jester A **jester** is a person who makes jokes. Long ago, kings and queens often had **jesters** to make them laugh.

Ll

listen **Listen** means to hear or try to hear. Most people like to **listen** to music.

loudly **Loudly** means done in a noisy way. The dog barked **loudly.**

loudly

Mm

moving If you are **moving**, you are going from one place to another. If something is **moving** along, it is getting better.

music The sounds made by a piano, a violin, and other instruments are **music**. The sound of a person singing is also **music**.

Nn

noise Noise means a sound we do not want to hear. Loud **noise** can wake you up.

noise

Oo

of course **Of course** means surely or certainly. **Of course** you will learn to read well.

often If something happens **often**, it happens many times. We **often** go to the movies together.

often

Pp

poems Poems are a kind of writing that is something like songs without any music. **Poems** often use rhyme.

posters Posters are large printed pieces of paper put up for everyone to see.

power   Power is energy that can do work. Running water can produce electric **power.**

props   **Props** are things used in a play, movie, or TV show.

Qq

quite   **Quite** can mean very. It is **quite** cold today. Dinner will be ready **quite** soon.

Rr

realized   If you **realized** something, you understood it clearly. We **realized** that she did a good job.

ruined   When something is **ruined**, it is spoiled completely. The bicycle was **ruined** in the accident.

ruined

Ss

scary   **Scary** means making someone feel afraid. He saw a **scary** movie.

shared   If you **shared** something, you used it with someone else. The twins **shared** a bedroom.

sharing   My brother and I are good at **sharing.**

sharing

shouldn't	**Shouldn't** means should not.
snow glory	A **snow glory** is a kind of flower.
stared	If you **stared** at something, you looked at it with your eyes wide open for a long time.
stood	If you **stood**, you were on your feet instead of sitting down. We **stood** in line for tickets.

stood

surprise	Something that happens that you did not plan is a **surprise**.

Tt

television	When you turn on a **television**, you can see pictures and hear sounds. You can watch shows on **television**.
toward	**Toward** means in the direction of. I walked **toward** home.

toward

Vv

visitor   A **visitor** is someone who goes to see places or people. The **visitors** from Italy asked us how to get to the hotel.

Ww

warmer   **Warmer** means more warm than something else. Summer is **warmer** than winter.

warmer

wherever   Please sit **wherever** you like. **Wherever** you want to go is fine with me.

whispered   If you **whispered**, you spoke very softly and low. I couldn't hear him when he **whispered.**

would   **Would** you like some candy? She said she **would** come to visit me.

wrong   **Wrong** means not right or not true. She gave the **wrong** answer.

wrote   The teacher **wrote** on the board. I **wrote** a poem about winter.

wrote

Writer's Handbook

Contents

Sentences

A **sentence** is a group of words that tells a complete idea. A sentence begins with a capital letter. Many sentences end with a **.**.
The pie is too hot to eat**.**

A **telling sentence** tells something.
It begins with a capital letter.
It ends with a **.**.
The girl lost her ring**.**

A **question** asks something.
A question is an asking sentence.
It begins with a capital letter.
It ends with a **?**.
Does Jill live on a farm**?**

An **exclamation** is a sentence that shows strong feelings.
An exclamation begins with a capital letter.
It ends with an **!**.
We can't wait to go to the circus**!**

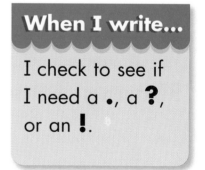

When I write...

I use telling sentences and asking sentences. Sometimes I use exclamations and commands.

When I write...

I check to see if I need a **.**, a **?**, or an **!**.

A **command** is a sentence that tells someone to do something.
A command begins with a capital letter. It ends with a .

Write your name on your paper**.**

Naming Parts

Every sentence has two parts.
It has a naming part and an action part.
The **naming part** names a person, animal, or thing.

The bird flies from the nest.

Action Parts

The **action part** of a sentence tells what a person, animal, or thing does.

The dog **chews on the bone.**

Word Order

The order of words tells what a sentence means.

The hat is on the cat.
The cat is on the hat.

Nouns

A **noun** is a word that names a person, place, animal, or thing.

The **apple** is red and juicy.

Nouns for One and More than One

Sometimes **–s** is added to the end of a noun.
An **–s** makes a noun mean more than one.

When I write...

I use nouns to give information.

Firefighters help keep us safe.

Sometimes **–es** is added to the end of a noun.
Add **–es** to nouns that end in **x**, **s**, **ch**, or **sh**.

Put the **boxes** on the porch.
The **benches** are in the sun.

Writing with Nouns

A noun can be in the naming part of a sentence.
A noun can be in the action part of a sentence.

naming part	action part
The **girl** Mary	cooked our **dinner.**

Verbs

A **verb** tells what a person, animal, or thing does. Many verbs are action words.

Mom **swims** on a team.

Verbs for One

Verbs tell what one person, animal, or thing does. Add –**s** to these verbs.

Dad **sings** to me.

Verbs for Two or More

Verbs may tell what two or more people, animals, or things do. Do not add –**s** to these verbs.

The boy and girl **skip** rope.

Verbs for Now and for the Past

Verbs can tell about action that takes place now.

Dad and I **wash** the car.

Verbs can tell about action that happened in the past. Add –**ed** to the verb.

Yesterday, I **helped** my mom.

When I write...

I use verbs to tell what is happening.

Is, Are, Was, Were

Use **is** and **are** to tell about now.

The sky **is** blue.
The clouds **are** white.

Use **was** and **were** to tell
about the past.

Tom **was** tired.
We **were** busy all day.

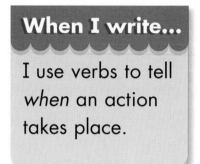

When I write...

I use verbs to tell
when an action
takes place.

Using the Word *Not*

The word **not** changes what a
sentence means.
A verb and the word **not** can be put
together. They make a shorter word
called a **contraction**. The letter **o** is left out.
An **'** is used in place of the letter **o.**

The fish **are not** hungry.
The fish **aren't** hungry.

Adjectives

An adjective is a word that tells more about a noun.
The **funny** clown led the parade.

An adjective can tell about color.

The **blue** room is my favorite.

An adjective can tell about shape.

The baby liked the **round** ball.

An adjective can tell about size.

Did you see the **big** tiger?

An adjective can tell what kind.

The **shiny** key fits the door.

An adjective can tell how many.

My sister has **twenty** marbles.

When I write...

I use adjectives to make word pictures.

Pronouns

A pronoun is a word that can take the place of a noun.
These words are pronouns.

I	you	he	she	it
we	you	they		

Pronouns can be used in the naming part of a sentence.
They are:

I	he	she	we	they

When I write...

I may use a noun in one sentence and a pronoun in the next. This makes my writing more interesting.

Tomás is in my class.
He is in my class.

Pronouns can be used in the action part of a sentence.
They are:

me	him	her	us	them

Lindy read to **the children**.
Lindy read to **us**.

Capital Letters

People and pets have special names. Special names begin with capital letters. The word *I* is always a capital letter.

My best friend is **Alex**.
I named my dog **Trooper**.

When I write...

I check to see if I need capital letters.

A title can come before the name of a person.
A title begins with a capital letter.
Some titles end with a **.**.

Our neighbor is **Ms.** Jane Kennedy.
Do you know **Judge Andy Smith?**

The names of days, months, and holidays begin with capital letters.

The **Fourth of July** is on a **Friday** this year.

Writing a Letter

Most letters have five parts.
They are the **date**, **greeting**, **body**, **closing**, and **signature.**
A **comma** , goes between the date and year.
A comma is also used after the greeting and closing.

- Read this friendly letter.
- Look for the five parts.
- Look for three commas.

Date	May 3, 200_
Greeting	Dear Bill,
Body	How are you? I hope you are better. I was sorry to hear that you broke your leg. I guess a lot of people trip over their cats. I hope you are getting around all right. See you soon!
Closing	Your friend ,
Signature	Ellen

Addressing an Envelope

Addressing an Envelope

After you write a letter, you can mail it.
Put the letter in an envelope.
Then seal the envelope.
Write your name and address in the
top left corner.
This is the **return address.**

Write the name and address of the
person you wrote to in the center of the
envelope. This is the **mailing address.**

Remember to put a stamp on your envelope.
Then it will be ready to mail.

Return
address

Ellen Lee
2610 Union St.
Glenview, IL 60025

Mailing
address

Bill Robins
2333 Sky Drive
Atlanta, GA 30301

Sharing a Book

Writing a book report is one way to
share a book.
Here is what you should
tell in your report.

- Title
- Author
- A little bit about the story
- One important thing that happens
  in the story
- Why you like the book – or don't
  like it

Here are some other ways to share a book.

- **Make a Book Cover**
  Draw a picture of a part you liked.
  Write the title and author of the book
  on your picture.

- **Be a Reporter**
  Be a radio or TV reporter.
  Tell about a favorite book.
  Tell why you liked it.

- **Act Out Your Book**
  Make stick puppets of characters
  in your book.
  With some friends, act out part of your book.

Spelling Lists

Bluebirds in the Garden
The Garden

1.	**far**	How **far** away is the sun?
2.	**car**	We can ride in Dad's **car**.
3.	**yard**	Our **yard** has many flowers.
4.	**dark**	Without lights the room is **dark**.
5.	**star**	Did you know that the sun is a **star**?
6.	**start**	Let's **start** the race.
7.	**sadly**	The dog howled **sadly**.
8.	**softly**	The snow fell **softly**.
9.	**work**	Mom and Dad go to **work**.
10.	**these**	**These** are my toys.

Jordan Makes a New Friend
Ice-Cold Birthday

1.	**born**	I was **born** in February.
2.	**fork**	Use a **fork** to eat the peas.
3.	**short**	My pants are too **short**.
4.	**for**	This book is **for** you.
5.	**or**	You may have pie **or** cake.
6.	**torn**	The newspaper was **torn**.
7.	**walked**	I **walked** to school.
8.	**sleeping**	The cat is **sleeping** on the sofa.
9.	**cold**	It is **cold** in winter.
10.	**would**	I **would** like more soup, please.

Do You Live in a Nest?

1.	**her**	The book belongs to **her**.
2.	**turn**	We each take a **turn** on the swings.
3.	**hurt**	I **hurt** my foot when I fell.
4.	**girl**	The **girl** has on a nice dress.
5.	**first**	I was **first** in line.
6.	**bird**	A **bird** sang outside my window.
7.	**slower**	A turtle is **slower** than a rabbit.
8.	**slowest**	A snail is the **slowest** insect.
9.	**once**	I read this story **once**.
10.	**which**	**Which** pencil is yours?

Fox on Stage

1.	**how**	**How** old are you?
2.	**now**	It is **now** springtime.
3.	**town**	A **town** is smaller than a city.
4.	**brown**	A **brown** horse ran in the meadow.
5.	**down**	Rain came **down** quickly.
6.	**clown**	A **clown** can be funny.
7.	**paper**	Dad reads the **paper** in the morning.
8.	**seven**	I will be **seven** on my next birthday.
9.	**pull**	Don't **pull** on that string.
10.	**goes**	He **goes** to work every day.

Doggy Art
The Snow Glory

1. **pretty** — That flower is **pretty**.
2. **little** — Your fish is very **little**.
3. **puppy** — My **puppy** likes to play.
4. **happy** — I am **happy** to be here.
5. **kitten** — The **kitten** played with the yarn.
6. **better** — I feel **better** now.
7. **about** — It is **about** time to go.
8. **round** — A football is not **round**.
9. **took** — I **took** a piece of pie.
10. **almost** — I was **almost** late.

I'll Join You
Leon and Bob

1. **cannot** — I **cannot** find my glasses.
2. **grandma** — My **grandma** makes the best rolls.
3. **popcorn** — We had **popcorn** for a snack.
4. **outside** — Let's play **outside** in the sun.
5. **something** — I have **something** to tell you.
6. **tiptoe** — Can you walk on **tiptoe**?
7. **boy** — The **boy** played football.
8. **toy** — I got a **toy** train for my birthday.
9. **school** — I like to learn at **school**.
10. **always** — Will you **always** be my friend?

Tested
Word List

Bluebirds in the Garden
The Garden

ground
much
shall
these
wish
work

Jordan Makes a New Friend
Ice-Cold Birthday

before
cold
full
off
would

Show Time: Your First Play
Do You Live in a Nest?

each
once
other
under
which

What's New in Mrs. Powell's Class?
Fox on Stage

along
goes
great
idea
pull

Doggy Art
The Snow Glory

almost
knew
picture
thought
took

I'll Join You
Leon and Bob

always
boy
move
open
school

Acknowledgments

Text
Page 18: "The Garden" from *Frog and Toad Together* by Arnold Lobel, pp. 18–29. Copyright © 1971, 1972 by Arnold Lobel. Reprinted by permission of HarperCollins Publishers, Inc.
Page 31: "Surco/Field Row" from *Gathering the Sun* by Alma Flor Ada, English translation by Rosa Zubizarreta. Text copyright © 1997 by Alma Flor Ada. Illustrations copyright © 1997 by Simon Silva. Used by permission of HarperCollins Publishers.
Page 44: *Ice-Cold Birthday* by Maryann Cocca-Leffler, pp. 4–32. Copyright © 1992 by Maryann Cocca-Leffler. Reprinted by permission of Grosset & Dunlap, Inc., a division of Penguin Putnam, Inc.
Page 70: "Sunflakes" from *Country Pie* by Frank Asch. Copyright © 1979 by Frank Asch. Used by permission of HarperCollins Publishers.
Page 112: "Fox on Stage" from *Fox on Stage* by James Marshall, pp. 34–48. Copyright © 1993 by the Estate of James Marshall. Reprinted by permission of Dial Books for Young Readers, a division of Penguin Putnam, Inc.
Page 132: © 1998 David McPhail
Page 140: "The Snow Glory" From *Henry and Mudge in Puddle Trouble*, text by Cynthia Rylant. Text copyright © 1987, by Cynthia Rylant. Reprinted with permission of Simon & Schuster Books for Young Readers, Simon & Schuster Children's Publishing Division.
Page 170: *Leon and Bob.* Copyright © 1997

by Simon James. Reprinted by permission of Candlewick Press Inc., Cambridge, MA, on behalf of Walker Books Ltd., London.
Page 191: "Making Friends" from *Nathaniel Talking* by Eloise Greenfield. Copyright © 1988 by Eloise Greenfield. Reprinted by permission of Scott Treimel New York.
Selected text and images in this book are copyrighted © 2002.

Artists
Meg Aubrey, 10–17
Arnold Lobel, 18–30
Glen T. Strock, 31
Mireille Levert, 32–35
C. D. Hullinger, 36–43
Maryann Cocca-Leffler, 44–69
Susan Spellman, 70–71
John Sandford, 72–75
Lee Lee Brazeal, 4–5, 84–101, 221
Martha Aviles, 102–105
Gil Ashby, 106–111
James Marshall, 112–127
Satoshi Kitamura, 128–131
David McPhail, 132–139
Suçie Stevenson, 140–147
Pamela Paulsrud, (calligraphy) 140
Benrei Huang, 158–161
Michele Noiset, 162–169, 222–223
Simon James, 170–190
Jan Spivey Gilchrist, 191
C.D. Hullinger, 192–195

John Sandford, 196–197
Franklin Hammond, 198–199

Photographs
Every effort has been made to secure permission and provide appropriate credit for photographic material. The publisher deeply regrets any omission and pledges to correct, in subsequent editions, errors called to its attention.
Unless otherwise acknowledged, all photographs are the property of Scott Foresman, a division of Pearson Education. Page abbreviations are as follows: (t) top, (b) bottom, (l) left, (r) right, (ins) inset, (s) spot, (bk) background.
Page 10 Kim Arnold (C) Courtesy of the family
Page 13 Kim Arnold (TC) Courtesy of the family
Page 15 Kim Arnold (TC) Courtesy of the family
Page 17 Kim Arnold (TC) Courtesy of the family
Page 30 (CL) Courtesy, HarperCollins Publishers/Photo: Ian Anderson
Page 156 (C) Courtesy, Simon and Schuster
Page 190 (TL) Courtesy, Candlewick Press
Page 202 (BL) PhotoDisc
Page 206 (BR) Artville
Page 206 (BR) PhotoDisc

Glossary
The contents of this glossary have been adapted from *My First Dictionary*. Copyright © 2000 by Scott, Foresman and Company, a division of Addison Wesley Educational Publishers, Inc.